Your Ultimate T
Travel Guide

Everything You Need to Know to
Enjoy Every Second in This South-
East Asian Gem

Table of Contents

Introduction - Why Thailand?

The Kingdom of Thailand, as it is better known, is one of the most visited countries on the planet. From backpackers to digital nomads, honeymooners to groups wanting fun in the sun, Thailand gives you everything you could possibly want, and just a little bit more besides.

Far from being just a sun-trap with touristic nightlife to enjoy, Thailand is packed with culture and traditions, and it isn't known as the Land of Smiles for no reason! The Thai people are welcoming, always smiling, and won't be able to do enough for you. This is just one reason why your time in this South East Asian country will be special from start to finish.

Despite that, there is a lot of background information you need to know before you even think about booking a vacation, or heading off exploring on your own steam. Thailand is an experience you'll never find anything to compare to, but it is also a country which is huge (513,120 square kilometres to be expect) so you need to know where to go, according to your needs and interests. From the sun-drenched islands in the south, the misty mountains of the north, Bangkok in-between, and the countless towns and cities besides, Thailand offers something for everyone.

This guide is going to tell you all you need to know before you decide which destination is for you.

We're also going to run through some basic information, such as currency, etc, and tell you how to get there and what you need to do in order to enter the country. There are also some useful tips later on in the book about what not to miss, but also what to make sure you avoid! Remember, there are parts of Thailand which are extremely touristic, and that means that the odd scam might come your way. Knowing what to expect will help you side-step them with ease.

So, why Thailand? Let's break it down.

- A friendly, welcoming country
- Packed with more areas of blinding natural beauty than we can even list
- Some of the best beaches on the planet
- Huge temples and areas of cultural significance to explore
- Wildlife in abundance
- Amazing snorkelling and diving opportunities
- The food - need we say more?
- An affordable location for all budgets
- A place to meet people from all over the world
- Fantastic weather
- Ancient ruins from long-gone civilisations
- Vibrant, varied nightlife

Surely that's enough to convince you?

Quick Facts About Thailand

Before we get into the things to see, the places to go, and all that fun stuff, we need to give you some basic information about Thailand. These are the facts which will form the basis of your stay, so it's important that you read them and memorise them wherever possible!

Overall, visiting Thailand is not going to be an alien or strange experience. Yes, this is a country which has a lot of differences to many other countries the world over, and a wonderful culture which is varied and unique, but it is also very used to visiting tourists from every corner of the globe, so you won't struggle to find the amenities and facilities that you need. If you forget something from back home, you'll find it in one of the countless 7 Eleven stores across the main tourist areas! If you're in Bangkok (definitely recommended) then you'll find all the big brand names in shopping, such as Apple, to name just one. You won't want for anything, and even if you visit a rural area, you're never too far away from a large town or city.

So, once more, let's break it down into quick and easy to digest facts about Thailand that you need to know.

- **Capital city** - Bangkok
- **Language** - Thai, but English is widely spoken in Bangkok and all tourist resorts
- **Religion** - Predominantly Buddhist

- **Currency - Thai Bhat**
- **Time zone** - +7 GMT. There is only one time zone across the whole of Thailand
- **Electricity** - 220 volts AC. It's unlikely you will ever be without electricity, but during the rainy season there might be the odd outrage
- **Dialling code** - +66
- **Wifi** - Widely available in all tourist resorts. You can also purchase a local SIM card to use with data from the airport or at a 7 Eleven store

It's always good to know a few random, fun facts too, so let's check some out.

- Thailand has two coastline - one on the Andaman Sea and one on the Gulf of Thailand
- The country is bordered by Cambodia, Myanmar, and Laos. It is possible to visit these countries, but you should check passport and border crossing information according to your country of origin first
- Thailand is the only country in SE Asia which has never been touched by a country in Europe, giving it a truly authentic feel when you visit
- You'll find both the smallest mammal in the world in Thailand - the tiny bumblebee bat
- The world's largest fish is the whale shark and it also calls Thailand home!
- Buddhist monks are hugely respected in Thailand and there was a time when all males were required to practice as a monk for a period of time. That isn't the case anymore
- Thailand is home to around 35,000 temples, so visiting a few is a must do

- The national flower is the orchid
- It is very hot in Bangkok during the summer months, and it has previously been named the hottest city in the world!
- Thailand used to be called Siam
- Siamese cats are actually from Thailand
- Thailand's mainland is huge, but it is also home to more than 1430 islands. Many of these aren't inhabited, but the huge tourist islands are extremely busy during the peak season
- Do not avoid street food in Thailand, it's often tastier than restaurant fare!
- A regular greeting is the iconic Thai bow, so be sure to practice it before you go
- Beware of the monkeys - more on that later!
- The island of Koh Phangan is home to the famous Full Moon Party - a must do!
- The climate varies hugely across the country and the islands themselves, so be sure to know when the best time is to visit. We'll cover that in more detail shortly

These are just a few fun facts to get your mouth watering at the idea of visiting Thailand. So, if you're ready and raring to go, let's get into the practical aspects of heading to this sun-drenched, friendly country.

Getting There & Visa Information

The first thing you need to arrange is a flight or some kind of transportation to get you to Thailand in the first place! You'll often find that the most expensive part of your vacation is without a doubt the flight, but after that, accommodation and the cost of living is super-low. Do not let the cost of a flight put you off, because you'll save cash when you arrive, and probably make up the extra money you paid in transportation.

You can make Thailand as expensive or cheap as you want to once you arrive, but one thing you shouldn't scrimp on is the length of your flight. You can save cash by flying indirect and catching connecting flights, but do bear in mind transit visa issues (depending on your country of origin) and the total length of travel time. Do you really want to arrive in Thailand wiped out and jet-lagged, needing two for three days to recover? Of course not! There is far too much to see and explore, so you need to be as fresh as possible when you arrive.

You'll find direct flights from most large cities the world over, and countless other indirect connections besides. The national airline is Thai Airways, but the big hitters in aviation all fly to Bangkok and the main tourist resorts, such as Krabi and the islands off the coastline. You'll find great deals with companies such as British Airways, Etihad, Turkish Airlines, Emirates, Qantas, Singapore Airlines, Royal Jordanian, Air France, KLM, and Qatar Airways to name just a few. There are countless more besides, so shop around for the cheapest flight you can find.

You can look at indirect flights to save cash, but also think about flying out of the peak season for cheaper fares. The weather will be slightly cooler, but you'll still be able to enjoy serious sunshine, regardless of the month. We'll talk about climate and the best time to visit in our next section! Try and find a flight into Bangkok and then a domestic flight to your main destination as another way to save costs.

Main Airports in Thailand

The main international airports in Thailand are:

- Suvarnabhumi Airport, Bangkok - The largest and busiest in the country. This airport is also used as a hub for domestic flights
- Don Mueang Airport, Bangkok
- Phuket International Airport
- Chiang Mai International Airport
- Samui Airport (for Koh Samui and other Thai islands)
- Chiang Rai International Airport
- Krabi Airport (also for some Thai islands)
- U-Tapao Rayong Pattaya International Airport

Whilst there are countless smaller airports around the country, these are the main ones you will find when looking for flights to the most touristic parts of Thailand. As before you, can also link to domestic airports from Bangkok in particular.

Visa Information

Whether or not you need a formal visa to enter Thailand completely depends upon your country of origin, your passport, and how long you intend to stay for. Visa rules change on a regular basis, so always check before you travel in terms of the most up to date visa regulations.

Overall, most visitors who arrive from western and Asian countries, such as America, Australia, New Zealand, South Africa, the UK, and other European countries do not need to arrange a visa beforehand. When you arrive in Thailand, your passport will be stamped and you are free to stay for up to 30 days. If you want to stay for longer, you will need to apply at the local visa office to extend your visa.

Again, check for your specific country of origin visa requirements, to avoid issues when you arrive in Thailand.

Weather & Climate - When to Visit

When to visit Thailand completely depends upon where you're going and how hot you can stand it! Because the country is so big, there are various weather systems which affect various parts of the country at any one time. If you want to avoid rain, you need to make sure you're not visiting your particular destination during the rainy season. Thailand is affected by monsoon seasons, so knowing about this before you start planning is key.

Of course, with today's climate change issues, we can never be 100% sure that a random storm won't affect a place it normally wouldn't out of season, but these are rare occurrences which cannot be planned for. Overall, Thailand is a year-around destination, but you do need to take rain into account at certain points.

To narrow it down, the best time to visit the main touristic areas is between the month of November, into the start of April. The wet season varies across the country, but between May or June into October you can expect most of the rain. August to October are the wettest months on average but if you head to the southern islands of Koh Samui and Koh Phangan during November and December, you'll probably notice rain, thanks to the pesky south-west monsoon.

Let's break it down month by month to make it clearer.

January - Good weather across the entire country, with little rain. The beaches on the west coastline are very sunny at this time, with cooler, more bearable temperatures. Koh Samui however is likely to be a little rainy.

February - The east coast might experience a few showers, but the rest of Thailand is hot and sunny with very little rain.

March - The heat begins to rise at this time of year, across the entire country. The beaches are starting to get busy also.

April - As with March, temperatures are rising the crowds are building across the entire country.

May - May is the start of the rainy season, however this is probably not going to become evident until the end of the month. Prices at this time of year are a little lower as a result, so it is a great time to visit, whilst still being very warm indeed. The east coast is probably the best spot for guaranteed sun and no rain.

June - Plenty of sun is still to be had and the rainy season is not in full swing, so you should only see a few showers at most. Once more, prices are low.

July - You'll notice the entire country is a little cooler during July, but the start of the month is a good time for those who like cooler (but still very warm) temperatures. You'll notice the rain picking up towards the end of the month, and more in the way of wind too.

August - Rainy season is in full swing, and if you're visiting the north, such as Chiang Mai, you'll notice this even more. Koh Samui is relatively dry at this time of year, compared to th rest of the country.

September - The wettest month of the year is September, but if you want to explore Bangkok and you're not too bothered about beaches, you might find a bargain at this time of year.

October - We're still in rainy season at this time, however less so than September. Temperatures aren't as high and humidity is lower, so this is still a good time to visit. The rain dwindles towards the end of the month.

November - Visitors start to pick up once again on the beaches, especially on the islands. The temperatures are warm but not searing, and the rain becomes less. Koh Samui is an island which often see a lot of rain during November however, despite the rest of the islands being relatively dry.

December - Once more, Koh Samui is a little rainy at this time, but everywhere else is warm and sunny, without much in the way of rain.

Overall, we should point out that the average temperature in Thailand across the year is a very warm 30 degrees C. Do not let the rainy season put you of visiting Thailand. Whilst rain can be quite heavy when it comes, it will disappear just as quickly as it started. There are many bargains to be had at this time of year also.

Important Dates For Your Diary

There are some fantastic celebrations across Thailand, and visiting during one of these occasions is a great way to learn more about the culture, whilst also having fun with a capital F!

Check out these dates for your diary and see if you can arrange your visit around them.

Chinese New Year (January or February, date varies) - Whilst not a specific holiday, there are still many celebrations which take place across the country. Head to Chinatown in Bangkok for a very memorable night out.

Chiang Mai Flower Festival (February) - Usually during the very first weekend of the month, the Chiang Mai Flower Festival in the north of the country spans for three days and is a celebration of the many beautiful flowers you find across the country.

Songkran (13-15 April) - If you want to get wet, this is the best time to visit! Songkran is a huge deal across Thailand and is a massive celebration. The official New Year in Thailand is celebrated by pouring water of everyone you see in the street. No, this isn't a random water fight, it is a symbol of washing away bad luck and sins, and welcoming in good luck and a fresh year.

Phuket Vegetarian Festival (October) - Spanning nine days, Phuket is home to the annual Vegetarian Festival. This is based on a Chinese tradition, and it is thought that abstaining from meat products for this time (the ninth month in the lunar calendar) will bring good luck.

Loy Krathong (November) - Mainly celebrated in the south-west of the country, you will see baskets made of banana trees, foam, or bread being set free along the river, with wishes being made as they cast them on their way. Again, this is to symbolise luck and good fortune.

Yee Peng (The Lantern Festival, November) - In Chiang Mai, thousands of people flock to watch countless lanterns being released into the night air, to celebrate the Lantern Festival, or the Festival of Lights.

Lopburi Monkey Festival (November) - If you're a monkey lover, head to Lopburi, just north of Bangkok, during November. You'll find a huge temple in the centre of town which the monkeys have claimed as their own. During this celebration, a huge amount of fruit and nuts are laid out for the monkeys to feast upon. It's great to see, but don't attempt to steal the monkeys' food, else you'll be in for a rather nasty fight!

Whilst it isn't mandatory to visit Thailand during a specific festival, it will certainly bring a little something extra to your time!

<u>Exploring Thailand, North to South</u>

We've already mentioned that Thailand is a large country, so it's important to know a little about geography, i.e. what is where! Distances across the country are very large, and if you want to explore more, and perhaps move around the country, you'll need to think carefully about how to get there. Luckily, we're going to talk more about that in a later section on how to get around Thailand with ease, both locally and nationally.

First things first, let's break Thailand up into distinct sections and learn more about what is where, and what you can see in each area.

Northern Thailand

The north of Thailand sits on the border with Myanmar, and it is home to those huge, iconic, misty mountains that everyone has seen on travel brochures and websites. This area of the country is extremely cultural, and this is the best place to learn about traditions, explore local food, and get to know the 'real' Thailand, away from the tourism boom of the southern islands.

Having said that, this part of Thailand is also home to Chiang Mai, which although still very cultural, is a place you will find people from all over the world. This spot is considered one of the cheapest places to live in the world, and as a result, you'll find backpackers and digital nomads mingling together, to give it a real international feel.

This part of the country is also home to some huge cave systems, which attract visitors throughout the dry season, hill tribes, as well as being part of the famous Golden Triangle.

If you are visiting this part of Thailand, try and avoid what is considered the 'smoky season', between February to April. This is when farmers burn back their crops and it often results in a rather smokey atmosphere which many people don't find pleasant.

A few highlights of Northern Thailand include:

Chiang Mai - A mountainous city which was once the capital of the Lanna Kingdom until 1558. The Old City is the best place to explore history and architecture, but you can't miss the huge and elaborate temples dotted around the city too. Some of the most famous include Was Chedi Luang, with its huge serpent carvings, and Was Phra Singh, dating back to the 14th century. We'll talk more about what to do and what not to do when visiting temples a little later in the book, but for now make sure you put these on your short list.

Chiang Mai is also a great spot for enjoying vibrant nightlife, with many bars, clubs, and cafes. In terms of an international feel and tourism, this is probably the only place in the north of the country where you will find it.

Chiang Rai - If elaborate temples are your thing then Chiang Rai is where you need to go. Chiang Rai sits on the border with Myanmar and Laos and it is home to the beautiful Way Phra Kaew, and the Mae Fah Luang Art and Culture Park, where you'll find artefacts dating back to the days of the Lanna Kingdom. Nearby you will also be able to explore the mysterious Mae Sai-Tham Luang Cave Complex, however do make sure that you do not venture too far inside and that you only visit during the dry season. These caves can be perilous out of the regular dry season, with rain flooding the inside.

Golden Triangle - Northern Thailand is part of the Golden Triangle, which encompasses the border areas of Thailand, Laos, and Myanmar. This is the part of the country where you will see the most in the way of stunning nature, and you'll get to experience the most authentic cultures. The name comes from the fact that the border areas basically form a triangle when you look at them from above.

Northern Thailand is a very easy part of the country to visit and thanks to the International feel of Chiang Mai in particular, it makes for a fantastic cultural break for those who perhaps need the safety net of tourism when visiting a country as 'different' as Thailand can be. If you want to push yourself away from the regular beaches and try something more authentic, Northern Thailand is a great choice.

Isaac - North-Eastern Thailand

Travellers who want to get a little off the beaten track should look towards Isaac. Probably not the most common choice for first time visitors, but if you are someone who likes to be more adventurous, then this part of the country will show you beauty and authenticity like nowhere else! The locals are very friendly to visitors who are keen to learn about their way of life, and if you love Thai food, this is the best spot to venture to!

Isaac encompasses the area which borders Vietnam and down toward Cambodia, and here you will find Khmer ruins in abundance. A few notable places to visit in this area include:

Nong Khai - Sitting on the banks of the Mekong River, Nong Khai is home to the Thai-Lao Friendship Bridge, which links Thailand with Laos and over towards the Laos capital. Be sure to visit the Sala Keoku Park, which is where you will find huge statues of various religious importance, including Buddhist, Hindu, and Christian figures. From there, venture over towards the Phu Wua Wildlife Sanctuary, where you'll find elephants, monkeys, and bears living in natural habitats.

Khon Kaen - Isaac is home to four large cities and Khon Kaen is one of them. Here you'll find a lot of modern fun to be had, but blended in with authentic Thai fare. Check out the Ton Tann Market for some authentic bargains to take back home, and the beautiful Way Thung Setthi temple, with its stunning white and gold exterior. You'll find some nightlife here and shopping also, and it's a great base for exploring the rest of the region.

Ubon Ratchathani - This is another large city in the Isaac, region and one which has many temples and ruins to explore. You'll find modern-day fare here also, but you'll find more in the way of culture than anything else. Be sure to visit Wat Phra That Nong Bua and Wat Maha Wanaram in particular.

You won't find many 'regular' tourists visiting the Isaac region, but you will find many adventurous travellers and backpackers. For those who want to really explore, this region is ideal.

Central Thailand

Most people stop off in Central Thailand, whether they stay there or not. This is because the central part of the country is where you will find Bangkok, a hugely important, cosmopolitan city, which is also the capital of the country. Central Thailand is also home to the lowlands and the central plains of Thailand and extends down to Kanchanaburi and Hua Hin on the coast of the Gulf of Thailand.

If you can, it's a great idea to spend a few days in Bangkok, perhaps before heading off to your main destination, probably an island towards the south. Bangkok has so much to see and do, and whilst it's certainly a very bustling and busy city, it is a true experience! Bangkok is also a very international place, so you will never feel too uncomfortable or lost if you're trying to find someone who speaks English, or if you're looking for 'regular' nightlife.

Hotspots in this part of Thailand include:

Bangkok - Definitely put Bangkok on your visit list. The main international airport is located here, so it is very easy to fly direct and then catch a domestic flight in a day or two, over to your main location. Bangkok has extremely vibrant nightlife, amazing street food, fantastic shopping, and it is also home to the stunning Grand Palace, the Temple of The Emerald Buddha and Wat Arun Ratchawararam. Khaosan Road is where you'll find shopping, nightlife, and many backpackers also.

Head to Chinatown during the Chinese New Year for a night you'll never forget, however most people tend to base themselves in Sukhumvit, to be close to the major tourism hotspots. The Skytrain (BTS) System is the perfect way to get around the city with relative ease.

Kanchanaburi - Visitors who are interested in history, particularly in World War II history, should certainly visit Kanchanaburi in this part of Thailand. The town is best known for the Death Railway. This is al one which was built during the war and crosses over the River Khwae Yai, encompassing the Death Railway Bridge. You'll find a museum which pays homage to those who died during the construction of the bridge and you'll also find the Kanchanaburi War Cemetery here, with countless Allied soldiers laid to rest.

Hua Hin - Located on the Gulf of Thailand, Hua Hin is a popular beach resort which is within very easy reach of Bangkok. You'll find the beaches packed during public holidays and weekends, thanks to its easy location from the capital, but it is also an idyllic place to soak up the sun. Kitesurfing is very popular here, and the seafood is to die for! You'll also find many upmarket hotels to stay, if you want a city and beach break between the two locations.

If you visit any part of Central Thailand, it will probably be Bangkok. This is a city which will give you whatever you ask for it, and whilst it is very international, it has that traditional Thai feel in many respects also. A few days in Bangkok will probably be enough, before venturing off to a beach or island location for the rest of your stay.

Eastern Thailand

The Eastern Thailand region is mainly made up of beach resorts, all of which are very easy to get to from Bangkok. As with Hua Hin, this means that they can get very busy with visiting locals during public holidays and weekends. There are also a few islands within this region, which sit within the Gulf of Thailand, such as Pattaya, Ko Samet, and Ko Chang. These are very popular island destinations for sun-seekers, and have beauty in abundance, although perhaps not as busy as the islands which sit towards the south. For that reason, if you're looking for a beach destination which is slightly less busy during peak season, these islands could be a good option.

Pattaya - Pattaya is home to the iconic Sanctuary of Truth, which is a must visit during your time on the island. This is a huge temple which is carved out of wood, and it is a truly magnificent sight. Pattaya has its own airport, which makes it very easy to get to from international destinations, but also from Bangkok, via a domestic flight.

Check out Jomtien Beach for a truly idyllic feel, with crystal clear water and white sand. Mini Siem is a great way to look around Thailand's main sights, without actually going in person! This is a small adventure park which has mini replicas of the country's most famous attractions. Of course, this being a tourism island, nightlife is very vibrant, and Walking Street is the best spot for fun and shopping.

Ko Samet - For those who want to chill out and enjoy nature, Ko Samet is a great choice. A relatively small island, you'll find stunning beaches to sit back and relax, such as Sai Kaew Beach and Wong Duean Beach. Wildlife and nature lovers should head to Khao Laem Ya-Mu Ko Samet National Park, which is a huge marine park with even more stunning beach spaces. Of course, there is plenty of nightlife here, although it tends to be a little slower and laid back, compared to other touristic islands.

Ko Chang - This is one of the largest islands you will find within the Gulf area, and it is home to some stunning jungle landscapes. You'll be able to venture into the jungle via a guided tour and spot wildlife and amazing sights before you. There are also many hiking trails and amazing waterfalls, like Kong Plu. There are some coral reefs just offshore also, for diving and scuba fans.

Most of the tourist attractions are located on the west coast of the island, however Ko Chang is more about nature and wildlife than it is about partying and touristic fun. For those who want to enjoy natural habitats, such as jungles, mangroves, and beaches, this is a fantastic island to choose.

We certainly haven't touched upon a huge amount of the main sights in these areas of Thailand, because there are far too many sights and attractions to mention. Remember, Thailand is a huge country, and this chapter is designed to help bring your attention to the various areas of the country, and where the main cities and towns are located. In our next chapter we will venture south, and explore the extremely popular islands and southern coastline of Thailand.

Southern Thailand And It's Islands

Without a doubt, the most common area to visit in the whole of Thailand is the southern portion, and the islands in particular. Whilst Bangkok is a hugely popular place, the islands are where the sun-seekers and party-goers head. Whilst there are plenty of opportunities for letting your hair down on the islands, such as the famous Full Moon Party on Ko Phangan, there are also many areas of cultural and natural beauty that you shouldn't miss out on.

It's impossible to talk about every island and what there is to see and do, so we will concentrate on three of the most popular - Ko Samui, Phuket, and Ko Phangan. To give you an idea of the sheer number of touristic southern islands there are in Thailand, here is a list of the main ones. Remember, there are also many other islands which are uninhabited too.

- Ko Samui
- Ko Tao
- Ko Phangan
- Ko Life
- Ko Yao Yai
- Ko Lanta
- Ko Phi Phi Le
- Ko Phi Phi Don
- Phuket
- Khao Phing Kan
- Ko Tarutao
- Ko Phayam

- Ko Nag
- Nang Yuan Island
- Ko Adang
- Ko He
- Ko Sukorn
- Ko Poda
- Ko Libong
- Ko Mai Phae

These islands sit on both the Gulf of Thailand and the Andaman Sea, depending upon their location. As we mentioned with our climate section, certain islands experience rain at certain times of the year, with Ko Samui being the one anomaly. The area also includes Krabi, which is on the mainland, but along the south coast. There are many beaches here also, and easy reach to island hopping opportunities.

Krabi - Located on the west coast of the southern portion of Thailand, Krabi is an extremely popular spot. Packed with areas of natural beauty, amazing beaches, and some cultural spots too, this is a great place to visit before heading off to visit a few of the nearby islands. You'll find huge limestone cliffs which soar high and drop down steeply into the sea, jungles, mangroves, wildlife, and even rock climbing in abundance, particularly at Railay Beach.

Aside from Railay Beach, which is only accessible by boat, Ao Nang is one of the most popular spots to visit. The beach here is divine, and there are many street food options and nightlife to enjoy.

From Krabi you can head off into the jungle and enjoy walking, trekking, and wildlife spotting. You will find elephant riding here, but it is always advisable to avoid this, as we will speak about a little later in the 'things not to do' section.

Koh Samui - One of the most popular islands in the whole of South East Asia, Koh Samui is a haven for those who want to party, those who want to enjoy nature, and those who love stunning beaches. This is the country's second largest island and sits on the Gulf of Thailand. The beaches are idyllic, with crystal clear water, white sand and palm trees, coconut palms, and huge mountains and rainforests in the background. Certainly one of the most beautiful places you'll ever visiting your life, Koh Samui is also home to the huge 12 metre tall Buddha statue at Wat Phra Yai Temple, made of gold.

Hotels in Koh Samui are a mixture of basic, jungle cabins, and huge hotels with upmarket spas. Honeymooners love Koh Samui, but so do backpackers and budget travellers too. Again, Koh Samui has its own airport, which makes visiting very easy.

Phuket - Phuket is Thailand's largest island and it is known for two very distinct things - beauty and partying. If you're looking for vibrant fun, Phuket is the place for you, but if you want nature to make your eyes water in the best possible way, Phuket is your ideal destination too.

Phuket sits in the Andaman Sea and it is covered partly in mountains and rainforests. You'll find some of the most popular beaches in the entire country on Phuket, and they are mostly found on the western side of the island. Head to Phuket City for some of the most colourful and lively nightlife around, but Patong is another destination on the island which is popular and worth a visit. You'll also find nightlife here, but this is more of a beach resort, with a laid-back vibe.

Phuket FantaSea is a popular place for families, and this is a huge theme park with regular fireworks, rides, attractions, and shows. For wildlife lovers however, it has to be Phuket Elephant Sanctuary. We will talk in more detail a little later about elephants and tourism, but this is one fo the few spots where you can visit them and know that they are being looked after and handled in the right way.

There is far too much to talk about in terms of things to see and do on Phuket, and this huge island should definitely be on your visit list. Again, this is a very international place, but not one for those who want to chill and relax in quiet and serenity!

Koh Phangan - This island is known predominantly for one thing - the world famous Full Moon Parties which are held every single month. If you've never been to a Full Moon Party, this is an experience you shouldn't miss, as it will certainly go down in your memory as something you'll never forget!

Boisterous, loud, busy, and quite alcoholic, this party is held on the south-eastern peninsula of the island, at Haad Rin. Sunrise Beach is the main focus of the parties, and you'll find many backpackers and general revellers enjoying the fun.

If you want to enjoy a more chilled out time however, simply avoid the full moon, or just don't go to the part of the island! The north is a good spot for chilling out, and yo'll find Hat Khuat and Hat Thian here, perfect for idyllic breaks in the sun. Head to Than Sadet-Ko Phangan National Park and Mu Koh Anything National Marine Park for nature and wildlife. These are two parks which are renowned for their natural beauty and wildlife, and spots not to miss.

No matter what the month, Southern Thailand and it's islands are always busy. The weather here is never particularly adverse, however Koh Samui can experience rain towards the end of the year. With temperatures averaging the 30 degree mark, it's no wonder so many people head to these islands and to the Krabi region for some relaxing fun in the sun.

Getting Around

Getting around Thailand can be categorised into two main areas - getting around the country and getting around regional areas.

Getting around the country can be done by air, bus, or rail. Long distances are best covered by air if you don't have the greatest amount of time. For instance, if you fly into Bangkok and want to spend a couple of nights exploring the capital, you can then catch a regional flight to any other part of the country, including Pattaya, Krabi, and some of the big islands in the south.

If you want to be more adventurous, you can try long distance coaches or rail. The railway system in Thailand is very high quality and it is one of the best ways to get around and see the scenery. You'll also get a very authentic experience for a low price too, especially if you travel between Bangkok and Chiang Mai on the train - amazing scenery! Long distance buses are a good alternative, however the scenery might not be as jaw-dropping as if you took the train.

Most visitors to Thailand for the purposes of tourism will tend to stick to either Bangkok of their destination, and that means regional travel is going to be more of a concern. If you're visiting the capital, the Skytrain (BTS) is a very quick and cheap way to get around the main parts of the city, or you can take the subway (MRT). Other options include a tuk tuk (expensive), a taxi, public buses or a motorcycle taxi. Most tourists will stick with the Skytrain option or a taxi, however tuk tuks are quite attractive for first time visitors.

A tuk tuk is three wheeled vehicle which is half car and half motorcycle and they are used to zip in and out of traffic and get you to where you need to be. These are a very authentic and traditional way of travelling, which means they're quite expensive and geared mostly towards tourists. Tuk tuks in Bangkok are known for being very pricey, however in resorts you'll probably find them a little cheaper.

You have a few options for transportation in regional areas:

Taxis
Tuk tuks
Buses
Ferries - In certain areas

Tuk tuks once again are always going to be the most expensive option for travel, but if you want to try one for authenticity's sake, you can give it a go. Most tuk tuk drivers will name the price, and whilst you can try and barter, you might not get it much lower. For that reason, taxis are often considered the best route. Again, make sure you ask how much it is going to cost and if they say they're going to use the metre, find out beforehand how much it should cost you. The old tourist scam of taking the scenic route to charge a higher price is alive and well in

Thailand's tourist areas! If there are several of you however, taxis do usually work out cheaper and faster.

Buses in and around the regional areas are very cheap and very convenient but not every tourist will feel comfortable because they might not know where they're going. Most drivers speak English, so it's something to just give a go! You'll save a lot of cash, and you'll get an authentic experience. Ferries are also an option if you want to cross large bodies of water, e.g. if you want to island hop. This is definitely something to try and it is a relatively cheap way of seeing the islands. Private boat tours will cost you a considerable amount, so if you can go the authentic way, you'll have a greater experience and you'll save cash.

Transportation around areas greatly depends on where you are, but these are the main types which are evident in most areas. Getting around Thailand certainly isn't difficult, and whilst it might seem overwhelming at first, remember this is a country which is very used to tourists from all over the world, and with a friendly and welcoming vibe, locals are more than happy to help out with any questions or queries on how to get around.

Experiences Not to Miss & Things to be Aware of

We can't list everything you should see and do in Thailand, because this guide would turn into a series of books that would never end! What we can do is highlight a few cultural areas which you should be putting on your to do list. The specific places to visit in every location are totally different depending on where you go, so once you've narrowed your destination down, spend plenty of time researching the hotspots and things of interest to you. There are far more than you will first realise!

Experiences Not to Miss

When visiting Thailand in general, there are a few things you should not miss.

Food, Glorious Food

There is one thing that Thailand is famous for internationally, and that is food. Thai food in a restaurant in a random city in the world might be wonderful, but in the country of its origin it is simply divine. Be sure to head to local restaurants to try authentic fare, and try and avoid the huge tourist restaurants if you want to find cheaper prices, and larger portions! Talk to a member of staff in your hotel and find out the places they recommend, and you'll have a more traditional and authentic experience as a result.

Another foodie area you shouldn't miss is street food. Don't worry, there is nothing dangerous about street food, provided you are sure it's been cooked well! Street food in Thailand is a way of life, so you're perfectly safe with all manner of delicious treats. Bangkok is the best spot to try all manner of meat, vegetarian, and seafood choices, as well as delicious sweet treats to try. You'll find indoor and outdoor street food markets all over the city, but in the more regional areas you'll also find street food to be a way of life. It's super-cheap and you can eat seafood you would normally pay a fortune for in a restaurant, for a mere fraction of the cost! Ao Nang's night market in Krabi is a great spot to try street food whilst shopping for bargains at the same time.

Visit The Elephants

Elephants a contentious subject in Thailand, and we'll talk more about why in a short while. For now, as part of the experiences you shouldn't miss, getting to visit elephants in a sanctuary is a great way to interact with these gentle giants. Phuket's Elephant Sanctuary is a safe place to visit elephants, as well as Chiang Mai Elephant Sanctuary.

Island Hopping & Boat Tours

If you have the time, make sure you do a spot of island hopping, or book a boat tour to take you to a few different islands. Many people fall foul of thinking that islands are all the same, but they're far from that! There are subtle differences and the landscapes are also varied, with some more jungle-based, others completely beach-based. Floating on the Gulf of Thailand or the Andaman Sea is also a fantastic experience, so make sure you get to see more than one island, and enjoy boat time during your stay.

Temples

Thailand is packed with temples and they are some of the most elaborate and beautiful buildings you'll ever see. Make sure you visit more than one during your stay, no matter where you are basing yourself. We'll cover temple etiquette in a short while, as there are a few things you need to know about how to visit and what not to do.

Speak to Locals

Thai people are amongst some of the friendliest in the world and they love to tell you stories about their land and their history. Sit and have a chat with a friendly local in your hotel or close to the beach and learn something new!

Beaches

It doesn't matter where you are staying, make sure to head to a beach at least once. Thailand's beaches are some of the best in the world, and for castaway vibes, you'll struggle to find better. Some beaches are busier than others, and it's best to avoid weekends and public holidays if you're visiting a beach close to Bangkok, and you want to chill to in quieter surroundings.

Scuba Diving and Snorkelling

There are countless spots for visiting the underwater residents of Thailand, and Phuket and Ko Phi Phi Islands are some of the best. In some cases, you don't even have to don a snorkel, you can simply walk out into the water knee high and you'll have colourful fish swimming around your legs!

Watch Muay Thai

Muay Thai boxing is famous and is centuries old. This is also Thailand's reversed national sport, so you have to watch a match! You'll find them all over the country, including Phuket, Bangkok, and Chiang Mai in particular. You could even learn a move or two at a Muay Thai school if you wanted to!

Things to be Aware of

The overwhelming majority of visits to Thailand are safe and wonderful, but there are things you need to bear in mind, just in case.

Temple Etiquette

Anyone can visit a temple, but there is a certain etiquette to bear in mind.

- Both sexes should cover shoulders and knees
- Take off your shoes
- Cover your ankles if at all possible, but certainly wear long shorts, or a skirt which goes blow the knees
- Do not wear vest tops or tank tops
- Keep your voice down and be respectful at all times
- Do not turn your back on an image or statue of Buddha - if you need to turn around, take yourself away from the image before turning around
- Do not point at an image or statue of Buddha
- Do not raise yourself higher than an image or statue of Buddha, e.g. to take pictures

Elephant Tourism

You'll see countless tour companies advertising elephant treks through the jungle and whilst that might sound like a fun thing to do, once in a lifetime even, these tours are often inhumane. The elephants in some cases have been sedated and work in very poor conditions. In order to stamp out elephant cruelty, it's best to avoid these tours altogether and instead stick to sanctuaries, such as the ones in Phuket or Chiang Mai, where you can interact and visit elephants in natural, playful environments. You'll feel good knowing that you did your bit for stamping out this inhumane tourism practice.

Monkey Bites

You'll find monkeys roaming free in many destinations, especially on the islands and coasts. This is normal, but do not be tempted to pet that monkey - they might look cute, but they have a temper and rather sharp teeth! Monkeys are also very inquisitive, so if they grab your bag strap, let them have a rummage around and they will drop it and walk away - don't try and wrestle it away otherwise they may become aggressive. When a monkey smiles at you, they are not smiling in fact, they are getting ready to attack! Monkey bites need to be addressed by a doctor, with injections and proper cleaning.

Don't worry too much about this issue however, if you leave monkeys alone, they will usually leave you alone too.

Interacting With Monks

You will see monks quite commonly in Thailand, and they will wear orange gowns and have a shaved head. Monks are highly respected figures in Thailand, but they are also nothing to be scared of, and are very friendly. You'll find many interaction groups with monks taking place, especially in Chiang Mai, where you can ask questions and learn more about Buddhism and culture in Thailand. It's customary to bow to a monk as a thank you, but the monk is not expected to do the same in return.

Never touch a monk, be respectful at all times, and do not try to shake hands, as this is not a customary thing to do.

Conclusion

And there we have it, your whistle-stop guide to Thailand, a beautiful, cultural, mysterious, and friendly country that everyone should visit at least once in their lives. Most people do not only visit once however, and usually go back time and time again.

There is far too much to see and do for a person to complete this within one visit, and the islands alone have activities which could span more than a two weeks' holiday. Learn as much as you can about the culture of Thailand before you visit and you'll gain so much from your time. Also be sure to gorge yourself on the delicious food and take as many photographs as you can.

For now, □□□□□□, or goodbye!

Impressum:

2019 Timo Schmid

1. Auflage

Kontakt: Timo Schmid

E-Mail: Timo.schmid@gmx.at

Covergestaltung: Lisa Biegemann

Coverfoto: Depositphoto

Haftungsausschluss:

Der Autor ist nicht haftbar für Verluste, die durch den Gebrauch dieser Informationen entstehen sollten. Der Inhalt dieses E-Books repräsentiert die persönliche Erfahrung und Meinung des Autors und dient nur dem Unterhaltungszweck. Der Inhalt sollte nicht mit medizinischer Hilfe verwechselt werden.

Die Nutzung dieses E-Books und die Umsetzung der darin enthaltenen Informationen, Anleitungen und Strategien erfolgen ausdrücklich auf eigenes Risiko. Der Autor kann für etwaige Unfälle und

Betreiber der jeweiligen Internetseiten verantwortlich. Zum Zeitpunkt der Verlinkung wurde die jeweilige Webseite auf Vereinbarkeit mit deutschem Recht überprüft. Verstöße gegen geltendes Recht wurden nicht festgestellt. Bei den verlinkten Webseiten handelt es sich um Inhalte Dritter, für die der Autor nicht verantwortlich ist. Eine regelmäßige Überprüfung der verlinkten Webseiten auf Rechtmäßigkeit kann der Autor ausdrücklich nicht leisten. Der Autor hat keinen Einfluss auf Gestaltung und Inhalte fremder Internetseiten. Diesbezüglich distanzieren sich Autor und Verlag von allen fremden Inhalten. Zum Zeitpunkt der Verwendung waren keinerlei illegale Inhalte auf den Webseiten vorhanden.

Hinweis: Aus Gründen der besseren Lesbarkeit wird auf die gleichzeitige Verwendung männlicher und weiblicher Sprachformen verzichtet. Sämtliche Personenbezeichnungen gelten gleichermaßen für beiderlei Geschlecht.

Kontakt:

Timo Schmid
Münzweg 4
9500 Villach

Printed in Great Britain
by Amazon

11350081R00031